D0962513

WESTMINSTER PUBLIC LIBRARY
3031 WEST 76th AVE.
WESTMINSTER, CO 80030

Also by Chris Fabry
Away With the Manger
Spiritually Correct Bedtime Stories

The 77 Habits of Highly Ineffective Christians

Chris Fabry

WESTMINSTER PUBLIC LIBRARY
3031 WEST 76th AVE.
WESTMINSTER, CO 80030

InterVarsity Press
Downers Grove, Illinois

©1997 by Christopher H. Fabry

All rights reserved. No part of this book may be reproduced in any form without
written permission from InterVarsity Press, P.O. Box 1400, Downers Grove, IL 60515.

InterVarsity Press® is the book-publishing division of InterVarsity Christian
Fellowship®, a student movement active on campus at hundreds of universities,
colleges and schools of nursing in the United States of America, and a member
movement of the International Fellowship of Evangelical Students. For information
about local and regional activities, write Public Relations Dept., InterVarsity
Christian Fellowship, 6400 Schroeder Rd., P.O. Box 7895, Madison, WI 53707-7895.

Published in association with the literary agency of Alive Communications, Inc., 1465
Kelly Johnson Blvd., Suite 320, Colorado Springs, Colorado 80920.

Cover illustration: Tim Nyberg

ISBN 0-8308-1963-0

Printed in the United States of America ♾

Library of Congress Cataloging-in-Publication Data

Fabry, Chris, 1961-
    The 77 habits of highly ineffective Christians / Chris Fabry.
        p.   cm.
    ISBN 0-8308-1963-0 (alk. paper)
    1. Christian life—Humor.   I. Title.
BV4501.2.F264   1997
248.4—dc21
                                                            96-50475
                                                                CIP

18 17 16 15 14 13 12 11 10 9 8 7 6 5 4 3 2 1
11 10 09 08 07 06 05 04 03 02 01 00 99 98 97

*An ineffective Christian
never remembers to thank anyone
under any circumstances.
Might as well learn that before
you begin this book.*

Preface

Not long ago I decided to take a break from all the conferences on excellence and spiritual success. I had been to seminars and dinners and week-long meetings that exhausted every conceivable topic concerning the Christian life. I went to men's meetings, couples' retreats, leadership training and Bible walk-throughs. I gathered countless notebooks and heard speakers who encouraged biblical success in business and life. I attended sports banquets featuring born-again athletes and coaches. To be honest, I was looking for a meeting whose title did not have the number 7 in it, something less stressful and frankly, not so spiritual.

Quite by accident I stumbled into a symposium called "The Quest for Mediocrity: A Modern Spiritual Paradigm." It was held in the ballroom of a seedy little hotel near Chicago. The carpeting was burnt orange, and the years of serving pressed chicken dinners had left a discernible pallor in the room. The speaker that day was Dr. Virgil Lacking, Professor of Lethargy in the Department of Indifference at Southwest Complacent State. It came as no surprise that his doctorate was honorary.

I found Dr. Lacking's approach so refreshing, so liberating to my soul, that during a break for lukewarm coffee I approached him and proposed this volume. Though he believed it to be a good idea, his penchant for languor caused frequent manuscript delays.

As the months dragged by in frustration, I decided to assemble this helpful volume myself using Dr. Lacking's unexceptional material. I have tried to write with his voice, with his lack of authority and with his ineffective style. The charts and artwork are reproduced from an independent recollection of his seminars. The 77 habits are adapted from notes found in wastebaskets and from a smattering of interviews Dr. Lacking gave over the years.

These 77 habits are by no means exhaustive of the many ways one may become ineffective in the Christian life, but I believe they represent the very best of the worst.

For study groups and personal enrichment, at the end of the explanation of each habit I have included questions, action points and, where applicable, Scriptures to avoid. These should aid in your quest for total spiritual impotence. There is a self-test at the end to take before and after reading so you may score your level of ineffectivity.

Of course if your desire is to be more effective in your spiritual life, if you yearn for a deeper walk with the God who made you, if you wish to live in a Christlike way with your family, friends and those around you, if you seriously desire discipleship, I suppose you could modify these habits and simply do the opposite of the advice listed here.

Whatever your desire—an average, normal, mediocre Christian life or a serious, self-denying, cross-bearing adventure—may this volume teach and spur you to the desired end.

Sola Mediocrum Ineffectum
(The misuse of Latin phrases is greatly encouraged by the author.)

Habit #1

Dichotomize Your Life

*T*RULY INEFFECTIVE Christians apportion their lives into secular and sacred components. They view spirituality as something done on specific days at specific times for specific reasons. The rest of their existence is unaffected by the "spiritual" realm.

This lifestyle is known as compartmentalization. You must strive to see church, worship, Bible study and religious activities as inherently spiritual, while you view everything else as secular.

Don't miss this opportunity to frolic in mediocrity. If you talk about your faith at work, if you memorize or read Scripture at times other than those prescribed for a religious interlude, or if you even think about spiritual themes during the secular compartment of life, you are not being ineffective.

If you see a beautiful sunrise while driving in your car pool, resist the urge to talk about the beauty of creation and the creativity of God—particularly if there are those in the car who believe in evolution. Never reference the other aspect of your compartmentalized life.

It is totally acceptable to pray, silently of course, about big work decisions, a pay raise or relational difficulties. This will make you feel like you're bringing yourself to the Almighty. However, you must squelch the urge to bring the smaller things to him, the everyday, mundane things. This would cause you to believe God is interested in all aspects of life. To be ineffective you must keep him at bay, distant from the totality of your existence.

Remember, your life is not something whole to present to God, only parts you control.

Scripture to Avoid: Romans 12:1

Habit #2

Make Tolerance Your God

*F*OLLOWING TRENDS in the culture will increase your ineffectivity. Study society closely and practice assiduously the trends you see. One current destroyer of the vital Christian life is tolerance.

It should be said that tolerance can be used for good, but in today's culture it has gone to an extreme, and extremes are very good.

You must, in your tolerance, accept anything and everything. Whether the issue is homosexual rights or funding for the arts, you must convince yourself that all viewpoints are not only valid but also equal. In this way you destroy the notion that there are absolutes. Tolerance taken to its logical end helps obliterate the fact that there is such a thing as truth and that we are bound to it and not our opinion polls.

Tolerate sin. Tolerate divergent opinion. Tolerate films that rewrite history. Tolerate perversion. Tolerate Elvis impersonators, if you possibly can.

In this resolve of accepting others no matter what they say or believe, you should perceive yourself as living a Christlike life, thereby confusing tolerance with love. You will then become popular with news organizations that look for sane, tolerant folks to juxtapose to the narrow-minded religious sorts who just don't want people to have any fun. If you get really good at it, you might run for public office.

Remember, society esteems tolerance for everything—except for those who hold to absolutes. They are intolerant, selfish and puritanical little sniveling . . . well, you get the point.

For Further Thought: What have you tolerated in others that goes against Christianity? What else could you tolerate that you haven't already?

Habit #3

Live in the Circle of Ineffectivity

*C*RUCIAL TO THE IDEA of spiritual squalor is the circle of ineffectivity. You see this lifestyle diagrammed below.

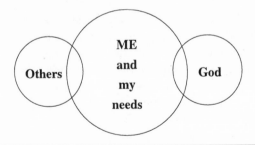

Figure 1

To live as ineffective as possible, put at the center of your life "Me and My Needs." This must always be paramount. You must never consider anything in any way other than how it will affect "Me and My Needs."

A Christian living a dynamic Christian life would, of course, have God as the center circle with "Me" being the smallest. You, however, must keep God to the side and make the spheres converge as little as possible, preferably on Sunday mornings or in emergency situations, such as when your flight takes a two-thousand-foot plunge while you're eating a fruit cup.

Likewise, keep "Others" outside your circle. The way you treat others shows how much you love God. The farther away you keep them, the farther you will be from him and the more ineffective you'll be.

Ineffective Exercise: Diagram your life with the above circles. Which is the largest? Do the circles intersect at all? Do you even need the other two circles? Discuss.

Habit #4

Never Be Content

*E*FFECTIVE CHRISTIANS are content, so you must strive for discontented living. Being content means achieving a certain state of peace with one's circumstances. Satisfaction. An ineffective Christian must never be satisfied.

On the physical level, you must not be content with your appearance. Lament your large nose, your thin lips and the gap between your teeth. Pine for a bigger brain or broader shoulders and do not focus on God's unique creation that is you.

Materially, you must not be content with your station in life. Always look at those who have more and condemn them for it. Thankfully, most Christians in the West are by nature discontent.

One of the key secrets to ineffective Christian living is an inner desire for more. It rips at the heart every waking moment. Make it yours. It doesn't matter what that "more" is. It could be a minivan with cup holders or a refrigerator with an ice-cube/fudge maker. It could even be something spiritual. I know many ineffective Christians who say they desire the "deeper life" but really want to see an angel by the expressway. They simply lack contentment with the spiritual experiences God has given them.

Be sure to cloak your lack of contentment in the shroud of excellence. Justify the never-ending search to fill the void of self by "aiming higher." We know the goal for much of this talk is simply self-gratification and indulgence. We work longer hours to make more money to buy more things that don't deliver, and we call this excellence.

Make discontent a part of your everyday life and you will become more and more ineffective.

Scripture to Avoid: Hebrews 13:5

Habit #5

Shun Pain

*I*F YOU ARE A Christian, it is inevitable that you will experience hardship and difficulty. Ineffective believers have learned the careful art of shunning pain.

In his infinite wisdom, the God of the universe puts pain in the path of his creatures. This draws them closer to him, causes them to rely on his strength and not their own, and helps them focus on heaven, where there will be no more pain.

Ineffective Christian living seeks to soothe and salve pain through artificial means. You may think that drugs and alcohol are the only ways to do this, but modern society has infinitely more resources. You can escape pain by watching television, listening to music, pouring yourself into your work or even getting involved in "religious" activities.

A physical problem is usually diagnosed when there is recurring pain. The malady can then be treated by a physician. Likewise, spiritual problems often come to the surface through the painful circumstances of life. If you simply ignore that pain, you will continually stunt your spiritual growth and thereby reach a higher plain of ineffectivity.

This is also true of others' pain. When someone else is hurting, this may cause a certain amount of identification for you. Do not allow them to pull you into this vicious cycle, because another person's pain can often cause you to analyze yourself. Simply say you'll be praying for them and watch a video or take a nap.

For whatever reason, pain seems to produce perseverance and a stronger faith in committed Christians. But for you, avoidance is the best method.

Ineffective Exercise: In order not to think of something painful in your past and how it has deepened your walk with God, write your own ineffective catchphrase such as "Shun Pain, Shun Gain." Repeat as often as necessary.

Habit #6

Base Your Faith Solely on Feelings & Experience

*H*OW DO YOU KNOW you are a Christian? For ineffective believers, the answer changes from day to day.

It is important to base your spiritual condition not on the finished work of Christ, but on feelings and experience.

If you have a relative who was near death on the operating table but saw a white light from the Great Beyond, use this as your proof of the afterlife. Base your salvation on any dream you have, particularly when you eat a pepperoni, anchovy and peanut-butter pizza just before going to bed.

Listen for the still, small voice that comes from a can of tuna. Watch for a sign from God in the lottery numbers.

You'll make much less of an impact on the world if you base your spirituality on feelings. One day you should fly high about the goodness of God over a recent raise. The next day be depressed because you need a new carburetor. This is part of the ebb and flow of an ineffective Christian. You're sure of God's love one day, confused the next.

Do not cultivate a depth to your Christian life. Instead seek warm fuzzy feelings toward God. Purchase a guitar and learn "Pass It On." Be prepared to smash the instrument when you mess up the Dm7 chord toward the end. Always say you believe the Bible, but trust in your experience and feelings.

Question to Ponder: What happened to you today that let you know you're a Christian or not a Christian?

Habit #7

Make Prayer Occasional

COMMUNICATION IS one of the most important aspects of any relationship, and that is why you should make prayer something occasional in your life.

If you were to see your union with God as something vital and living, you would desire constant communication. After all, to know you can speak to the King of Kings at a moment's notice is truly a staggering thought.

But ineffective Christian living will make this communi-

18

cation sporadic, or simply an option that's tacked on at dinner and during worship services.

As I've said earlier in this volume, you should pray only about the large decisions in life, like who to marry, what college to attend and whether to get tinted glass in your minivan. But true mediocrity demands even less. What you must actually do is make up your mind about the decision that faces you, and then subtly conform the will of the Almighty to your own. This not only justifies whatever choice you make but also makes you feel spiritual since you can rightly say, "I prayed about it."

Prayer should be something that comes not from the heart but from the head. You must pray the same things, the same phrases over and over, for this will make you more comfortable, and comfort is always the goal of the ineffective Christian. During the worship service it is fine to bow or even kneel, but your mind must not be on the words you are praying but on the mental images of your ballgame, your dinner or the department store you could visit while the kids are in Sunday school.

Since you think about so many other things when you pray, keep your prayers short and to the point. "I want _____ and ____. In Jesus' name, Amen."

Scripture to Avoid: 1 Thessalonians 5:17

Ineffective Hymn:

Sweet Minute of Prayer

Sweet minute of prayer, sweet minute of prayer,
That's just about all that I can spare.
I have regrets and lots of sin
So I'll see if I can squeeze them in.
In sea-sons of dis-tress and grief
My greatest prayer is quick relief.
But things are swell, I've no despair,
I'll just spend half a minute in prayer.

Habit #8

Major on the Minors

SINCE THE WHOLE topic of faith is so nebulous, so hard to grasp, the ineffective Christian must choose two or three issues and cling to them ferociously. While this clinging does very little for your spirituality, it will make you feel like a Christian, and feelings are everything when you want to be ineffective.

You must focus your daily gaze on these chosen points, rather than on God's grace and the whole counsel of his Word. The subjects you identify with not only will make you feel like a righteous person but also will help you judge others.

For example, focus your faith on the rapture and the end times. Or home schooling. Or tongues. Women must submit to wearing dresses with small floral prints on every odd-numbered Sunday.

What you choose as your issue is not as important as how tightly you hold to it. Of course you cannot use as your points specific scriptural verities like the sinlessness of Christ, the virgin birth or the resurrection. You must choose something obscure enough in Scripture that there is disagreement in the body. This will further divide believers and keep them fighting among themselves rather than making an impact on the world, so you've not only kept yourself ineffective but spread the mediocrity around.

Discussion Question: What is the litmus test by which you judge another person's Christianity? Choose now if you don't have one:

1. Age of earth
2. Author of Hebrews
3. Age of author of Hebrews

4. Location of Noah's ark
5. Type of fruit eaten in the Garden of Eden
6. Moses' sandal size

Habit #9

Strive for Imbalance

YOU MUST GO ONE step further if you desire the ineffective Christian life. Simply put, you should strive for an uneven keel. Live off balance. Your ship of faith must continually list.

This means you don't stop at majoring on the minors. Continue to practice unbalanced living at every turn.

Focus on your family so much that both parents quit working. Decide you can't really be good parents if you don't spend every waking moment of the day protecting your children and training them. Or become so involved in work and career that you forget you even have children.

Read only fiction. Lose yourself in a fantasy world of made-up Christian characters who fight angels or move west. Or get lost in the world of the "real." People who think only nonfiction can be "true" live dreadfully uncreative lives.

Do not take Scripture as a whole, comparing verses and passages. Treat each phrase independently from the rest. This will allow you, for example, to justify your "prayer only" method of healing by a passage in James when God has provided a perfectly good shot of penicillin from the HMO you declined at the office.

Imbalanced living will further marginalize you from the rest of the world. By going overboard you can take even something that was created good and turn it into a tool for ineffectivity.

Question to Ponder: In what ways are you living an unbalanced life today? How can you make your ship of faith list further?

Habit #10

Be a Hearer Only

*I*T MAY SURPRISE you that some of the most ineffective Christians today learn more about the Bible than anyone else. Let me explain.

Those who constantly sit under the teaching of the Word have a wonderful opportunity for mediocrity. These are people who most likely have five or more Bibles as well as a shelf of Christian books and commentaries, and say "Amen" while listening to their Christian radio station (with all car windows down, volume up). These people teach classes, answer questions correctly and pray an inordinately long time on Wednesday evening.

But the pivotal word for them is *hear,* for they only listen to the Word and don't do it in their lives. Follow their example. Become filled with the desire to hear facts and view charts and maps about the Bible so you can tell others all the neat information you've gleaned.

But do not *do* the Word. Go away from each conference or seminar feeling very good about transcribing the entire outline and all the scriptural references, but don't do a thing about changing your own life.

If you encounter an admonition against a particular sin, simply look past the passage until you come to something you're already doing right. This, of course, is like a man who looks in the mirror at a restaurant and fails to remove the broccoli lodged between his teeth, but is quick to point out the creamed corn on his neighbor's lapel.

Hear as much about Christianity as you can, but do as little as possible so it will have the least effect in your own life.

Scripture to Avoid: James 1:23-25

Habit #11

Be a Spiritual Sponge

*T*HERE IS ANOTHER component to "hearing" the Word that will make you even more ineffective. As stated, some hear the Word and do nothing about their own life. But spiritual sponges provide an alternate means to mediocrity.

Spiritual sponges, like the hearer, show up at every service, take notes on sermons, memorize verses, attend retreats, buy Christian books galore and subscribe to every Christian magazine and devotional.

Spiritual sponges know all the kings of the Old Testament. In alphabetical order. Spiritual sponges know the diet of the prophets, how many calories are in a locust and how much the ark would cost today if built with original materials. Spiritual sponges desire the true trivia of the Word.

Unlike "hearers," spiritual sponges are open to correction and will change sinful habits and behaviors in their lives. What spiritual sponges do not do is use their knowledge to help others. They will not teach a class. They will not present themselves for leadership in the church. They won't drive a bus or take the offering, and most of all, they will not engage anyone outside the church in meaningful conversation regarding what they know.

Call them shy, call them intellectual, call them introspective. Just don't call on them to pray out loud during a service. If you must learn more about the Bible and the Christian life, make sure you imitate the spiritual sponge, and you will be filled with lots of knowledge but empty of concern for others.

Action Point: What bit of biblical knowledge that could change a life can you keep to yourself today?

Habit #12

Provoke Your Children to Wrath

*O*NE OF THE GREAT ways to display a defective faith is the way you treat your children. Everyone knows how vexing it is for the little termites to see your inconsistency lived out before them. The good news is, you can do even more damage.

Provoke them. Poke them with your words. Never let them feel they are accepted or that the job they do is good enough.

If, when they are young, they are told to make their beds, tell them they did a fine job while you quickly tuck and fluff. This lets them know their effort just wasn't up to your standards.

Find the one patch of grass they didn't cut. Criticize their best friend with the squirrel-tooth earring. Focus on the B in math. Make fun of their favorite music group and say, "They sound like a bunch of mistreated laboratory animals."

Start your sentences with the phrase "When I was your age . . ." Never, under any circumstances, apologize or admit you are wrong in their presence.

Above all, do not treat them as the unique beings God created them to be, but make them conform to your tastes, your desires and preferences. This will smother creativity and mold them to your likeness rather than the heavenly Father's.

Vex them to the point that they clench their teeth and run screaming to their rooms once each day, then reassure yourself that this treatment builds character. Remember, an ineffective parent can make anything seem right.

Question to Ponder: How were you provoked to wrath as a child? In what ways can you replicate that behavior today?

Habit #13

Be Thankless

*I*N ALL MY YEARS OF analyzing truly ineffective Christians, I have yet to find one who has been thankful for anything. This is a hallmark of spiritual inadequacy.

If you were to sit down right now and list the blessings in your life, no matter what circumstance you are in, you would no doubt need reams of paper and a stack of pencils. This is why I say never, ever sit down and list the blessings in your life. It can only lead to thankfulness, which you must spurn.

Do not be thankful for God's faithfulness. If you see a miraculous answer to prayer, quickly forget it. Do not record it or tell others about God's goodness.

Do not be thankful for current material blessings like a roof over your head and food on the table. Do not compare yourself with those in the world who do not have such blessings. Instead compare yourself with the few who have bigger dwellings with better furniture and more attic space.

Do not be thankful for your spiritual blessings. Do not be thankful for God's Word, but whine that you would rather live in Old Testament days when you could hear the audible voice of God.

If you are single, desire a spouse and do not be thankful for the freedom you have. If you are married, pine for singleness and do not be thankful for the provision God has given you.

Remember, it is much easier to keep the fire of thankless-ness going when you stoke it with an attitude of ingratitude.

Action Point: Make a list of the things you're not thankful for today and share them with a friend.

Ineffective Hymn:
Count Your Problems
When upon life's pillows you are lying down,
When you are in comfort and without a frown,
Add up all the negatives you think you see,
And you'll be surprised at just how mad you'll be.
Count your problems, name them one by one.
Count your problems, scorn what God has done.
Count your many problems, make the list real long.
Count your many problems while you sing this song.

Habit #14
Get to the Head Table

*I*F YOU ARE SERIOUS about being an ineffective Christian, you must seek to be served.

Others no doubt are under the faulty assumption that you are their equal. At every turn you must show others how important you really are. Desire to be at the head table with the important people. At work, let others know you were the one who came up with the good idea first. When it is time to clean the bathroom or scrape the mashed peas from the kitchen floor, have your spouse or children do it. This lets them know you are much more important.

Seek the up-front positions in church so that those in the

congregation will know how truly gifted you are. Never seek a job like setting up chairs or scraping the dried Cheerios from the nursery floor. These carry no glory, and your efforts may go unnoticed or unrewarded. An ineffective Christian always strives for recognition.

Do not become a follower or a disciple. You must show people you desire to lead and will not be satisfied with any lesser role.

Seek applause. Gravitate to the spotlight. Use every opportunity to let others know they should bow down to you. And when they do applaud and praise your abilities with fervor, wave them off and eschew their worship. This will cause others to see you as a truly humble person and will give them even more reason to serve you.

Question to Ponder: In what ways have I sought to be served in the last week? How can I be better served? Who can I get to scrape peas today? Why are there so many Cheerios in the nursery anyway?

Habit #15

Live an Unexamined Life

YOU WILL ENTER A NEW sphere of ineffectivity if you live life unexamined. For maximum effect, stop all analysis of your relationship with your Creator. This can be achieved in a number of ways.

First, busy yourself. Keep yourself so busy you don't have time to think about life's purpose, the eternal destiny of those around you and what legacy you'll leave behind. Shut out all thoughts of the brevity of life. If someone talks about death, change the subject to more "positive" things. Never discuss the afterlife. Live for the moment, not eternity.

Second, the greatest companion of a busy life is a crowded life. Crowd it with friendly chatter and talk of the weather and how it seems to be much colder this year than last. Crowd your life with scheduled events that keep you moving from one to the other until you are living on automatic.

Third, resist the temptation to look at your motives, the "why" of what you do. Live as if you cleared that up years ago. You will become shallow, which is the byproduct of a busy life.

To live unexamined means each time a thought enters your mind about the cross, the crucified life, whether you're making your own comfort and security your god, you must immediately push it out.

Honestly, dwelling on this chapter much longer is not a good idea. Go out there and live. Be happy. Fulfill yourself. And for mediocrity's sake, stop thinking about it!

Scripture to Avoid: Psalm 139:23

Habit #16

Avoid Close Relationships

*I*F YOU WERE TO skip all the other habits found in this volume and cultivate only this one, you would still be classified as "highly ineffective," so avoid close relationships.

Those who would be lukewarm in their faith must keep others at a distance. Do not confess your sin to another person. Never divulge your deepest thoughts and longings. Do not open up or let yourself be the recipient of such talk. Never be there for another person, for you may be strangely drawn to the growth it produces.

If you would have lots of surface relationships, you must learn to say, "Hi, how's it goin'?" and not ever actually mean it. You should only mean *I am saying a polite hello to you so that I can move on to some other surface relationship very quickly, so please just say "Fine, how are you?" and I'll be on my way.*

Of course God wants you to have deep relationships on the horizontal plane (with people) so that you can deepen your relationship with him on the vertical plane. He often puts people in your life to knock off the rough edges. God confronts you with others and uses you to confront. He loves you with other people and uses them in your life.

My best advice is to just avoid people as much as possible.

Questions to Ponder: Who on earth knows you best and desires a closer relationship with you? Do not return their phone call. Distance yourself from this person today.

Habit #17

Treat God like a Pal

ALMIGHTY. OMNIPOTENT. The Great I Am. Awesome Lord.

These are terms you must not use or think about if you are to maximize your ineffectivity. Do not exalt God as Lord over all in your life. Instead you must bring him down to your own level. You must think of God as your heavenly pal.

The Good Lord. The man upstairs. My Big Buddy. Mr. Jesus.

You must take the gospel song "What a Friend We Have in Jesus" to the extreme. When you are tempted to sin, do not picture God sitting on his throne, surrounded by worshiping angels and beings too wonderful to describe. Do not picture him in his blinding righteousness, or yourself filled with awe as you shrink from his presence.

Picture him in a cardigan and jeans, putting his arm around you and saying, "Hey, that's okay, bud. Don't sweat the little sins, I'll take care of it." By doing this you will treat the sacrifice he made on the cross as something one business partner would do for another.

Think of God as a loving, doting grandfather, complete with rocking chair and beard. Pray casually, and without reverence, beginning your prayers with something like "Hi God, it's me."

If you focus your mind on making the Almighty, Omnipotent Master of the Universe seem like any other person, you will be well on your way to a wonderfully ineffective life.

Introspection Corner: How have you treated the Big Guy like a pal this week?

Habit #18

Squelch "the Dream"

*T*O BE INEFFECTIVE, you must strive for stagnant living. One of the best ways to accomplish this is to quell all efforts at "the dream."

I define "the dream" as your God-given, nagging sense of purpose. For some it is writing, for others the dream is becoming a pastor or teacher or evangelist, and for others it is simply getting the kids dressed and to church on time, though this is more "the wish" than "the dream" in our house.

"The dream" keeps coming back to you, as if God were pushing you toward an ultimate goal. No matter what you do you can't stop thinking about it: starting a ministry to a specific group, beginning an outreach to neighbors, or starting your own business to spend more time with the family.

You must fight these little whispers from the Almighty. You must tell yourself that it probably wouldn't work and nobody would come or it would cost too much money.

Keep "the dream" to yourself, because verbalizing it, even to the closest ones around you, can be deadly. They might think it a perfectly good idea and encourage you. If you do let it out, make sure you surround yourself with those whose spiritual gift is discouragement. Embrace those who will laugh and tell you how silly it is for someone like you to have such thoughts.

To live ineffectively, kill your dreams one by one, and you will be a slow-moving stream filled with stagnant water.

Action Point: Write your dream on a piece of paper and tear it into tiny bits. Repeat as often as necessary until you can't remember what it was.

Habit #19

Be Negative

SOME CHRISTIANS seem to always see the glass half full, find the silver lining behind every dark cloud and make lemonade from life's lemons. If you want to be ineffective, you must get far away from these people and seek to live negatively.

You may think I am talking about the obvious ways to demonstrate a negative attitude. Believe me, there are a million small avenues to help spread dread every day.

First, the weather. Complain that it's either too hot or too cold, too wet or too dry. If you go through a snowy winter with little sun, complain about it. Then on the first really warm day of spring tell others how hot you are.

A negative attitude starts with things you can't change such as the weather, your spouse and your children, and moves to things you can change such as your lawn, your breath and your grade point average. Half the fun of being a negative person is pointing out the flaw in things you could actually change. Because of your stubbornness or laziness, you don't, and that's great.

A negative attitude begins in the morning, when you first awaken to the new day. If there is any part of you, deep inside, that smiles at the opportunities that are ahead, you must immediately focus on how early it is or how late you are or how awful you look or how much weight you ought to lose.

Being negative is only a thought away, and it's a great avenue that connects you with the ineffective highway.

Nega-Quiz: On a scale of 1 to 10, how negative are you? Support your answer with examples. Ask others how you might be more negative today. Complain about the length of this quiz to a friend.

Habit #20

Seek the Quick, Self-Help Solution

*I*F YOU'VE BEEN A Christian for any amount of time, you know life can be very difficult. For some reason God does not take rough situations from you but seems to add problems. The ineffective Christian, in those days of tumult, will seek to alleviate the difficulty with books and radio call-ins that promise a ten-step solution.

The following is my own four-step solution as an example:

Step 1. Recognize you have a problem and start looking for anyone with easy answers. The first person or book that promises a painless outcome should be trusted—or for those with financial problems, the cheapest seminar.

Step 2. Find someone who will give specific directions to alleviate your problem. These guidelines should not be nebulous like "Pray about it" or "Consider what Scripture has to say on the subject." Rather, they should be quite pointed, like "Declare bankruptcy now" or "Throw your teenager into the street tonight."

Step 3. Make your decision without consulting any trusted friends who know and care for you. People like this only get in the way and have a tendency to drag the problem out for days and even weeks.

Step 4. Trust your instincts. After you've made your rash decision, lean on your own understanding. Remember, God loves those who self-help themselves.

Christians who seek to make life easy will be the most ineffective in the long run. The rule of thumb is, seek a solution, not God.

Introspection Corner: Describe a time in your life when you didn't seek quick answers. How would you be different today had you followed a ten-step process?

Habit #21

Live a Homogenized Faith

*I*T IS PIVOTAL THAT you seek stunted spiritual growth to keep your ineffectivity at a maximum level. One way to accomplish this is to live "homogenized." By this I mean you must only drink in the milk of the Word.

Learn John 3:16 and be able to recite it clearly, but have no idea what the surrounding verses say or what context it's in. If someone asks a tough theological question on an unrelated subject, respond, "Well, John 3:16 says . . ." Make John 3:16 the exclusive passage of your life that answers everything, and always recite it with a vacant smile.

Demand a Bible with lots of pictures in it. Focus on the chapters that are illustrated with the most vibrant colors.

At times you will be challenged to look at other parts of Scripture and think. As much as it lies within you, daydream. Think of love and harps and clouds and all the fun you'll have in heaven. But if you must read, emphasize the love of God in those passages and skip over the attributes of righteousness or holiness or justice.

If you saturate yourself with milk at the exclusion of meat, you will remain childish in your faith and make a very small impression on the world.

Verse to Read: 1 Peter 2:2a. Read the first part of the verse, then draw a picture of God's love with the crayon of your choice. (Remember to use the whole page and try to color in the lines.)

Habit #22
Make Music the BIG Issue

As stated earlier, the unexceptional believer finds one issue and bases their life calling on it. Because music is so controversial, there is no better focus.

Music can stir the soul. It can explain theological truths and plumb the depths of subjects like grace, mercy and the grandeur of God. Ineffective Christians take this wonderful gift and use it to divide.

Some may advocate singing only hymns written before 1800. Others will further segment the hymnal and insist on up-tempo tunes like "He Lives" and "Wonderful Grace of Jesus" in the morning service and "Like a River Glorious" in the evening. Another person may threaten to leave the congregation if you don't sing "In the Garden" at least once a quarter.

On the other side are those who enjoy praise choruses or the latest worship tunes they learned at weekend conferences. Your favorites should include particularly repetitive songs like "Sing Alleluia" or those that change only a few words like "Alleluia."

It is imperative that you not in any way seek a balance between these two extremes. You must not appreciate differing styles of music, different instruments or ways of expressing praise. Stay narrow. Stay focused.

Do not quibble over the words of the text; this actually shows signs of maturity and that you're analyzing what you're singing. Instead base your musical taste only on style. This ensures discord in the body and ineffective living for you.

For Further Reflection: Take a moment and sing through the hymn that follows.

Hymn for the Ineffective Christian
(sung to the tune "Nettleton," or "Come, Thou Fount")
Come, thou Fount of ev'ry blessing,
Give me what I want today;
Entertainment never ceasing,
Paths of comfort line my way.
Teach me nothing that will make me grow,
I want to stay right where I am;
True meat comes from your Word, I know,
But I crave spiritual SPAM.

I try hard to lead a good life,
I recycle, clean my feet.
I buy presents for my good wife,
Help old ladies cross the street.
I have quit my game of poker
And I'm trusting you'll be glad.
My life is so mediocre,
But I'm really not that bad.

O to self how much I'm focused,
Daily I'm constrained to be!
You give manna, I choose locust,
And the world revolves 'round me.
Prone to squander love, so infinite,
To forget my loving Lord.
Take an hour, no, take two minutes,
That's all that I can afford.

Chorus of Mediocrity (sung to "Alleluia")

In-ef-fect-ive	(8 times)
Living for self	(8 times)
Meet my needs now	(8 times)
Make me hap-py	(8 times)
In-ef-fect-ive	(8 times)

Habit #23

Cultivate Worry

*C*ULTIVATE WORRY like a garden. To be fully ineffective you must till the soil of worry and plant seeds of angst. Angst will take root and bring forth fear, which is simply worry on steroids.

You must worry about the little things of life. Will there be enough antifreeze for the car? Will your aluminum siding last a full twenty years? Worry about choices. Which dinner to make. Which bank to choose. What toaster to buy. Which professor to take for pivotal courses such as "Medieval Indo-European Macramé Patterns" or "The Influence of *Gilligan's Island* on Greco-Roman Mud Wrestling." Worry about making mistakes, even when all options available are good ones.

You must worry particularly about things you have virtually no control over. Let worry control you, vex you and hound your every step. If you have a difficult task, do not spend time planning; simply worry, and spread it to those around you.

Never pray about the object of your worry, because this might cause you to put things in perspective. Do not reflect on the awesome God you serve.

Do not learn from your past. It's probably true that the very thing you're worrying about has some correlation to a worry you've experienced before that turned out to be nothing to worry about. Resist the temptation to remember, and thus continue worrying.

Above all, do not exercise faith, because faith is the antithesis of anxiety. Focus on yourself, for this is the raison d'être of worry. (Worry about spelling *raison d'être* correctly as well.)

If you're concerned that you are not as ineffective as you should be after reading this book, follow my advice and worry about it.

Scriptures to Avoid: Philippians 4:6; Matthew 6:25-34

Habit #24

Be a High-Maintenance Believer

ONE WAY TO BE ineffective and stay that way is to live a high-maintenance Christianity. This works well in your relationship to God and others.

By "high-maintenance" I mean that you cannot do anything independently. You constantly are looking to God and others for help and direction in areas that really need no clarification. Every detail of life has to be mapped out and signed in triplicate before you act.

In your relationship to others at church you must expect unbelievable levels of communication. You should always have a question about the music chosen by the choir. You should always raise your hand in Sunday school and harp on the typeface the office staff chose for the bulletin.

A cursory look at the high-maintenance Christian might lead you to believe they really are dependent upon God because they seem to consult him at every turn. In truth, people in this category are not really concerned about what God wants from them. Rather, they veil their own desires in continual clarifications so that in the end they get their own way.

Being high-maintenance can lead you to new levels of ineffectivity as you require more and more people to meet your every need. Remember, the more you make others center around you (refer to circle of ineffectivity on page 13), the more ineffective you become as a follower of Christ.

For Further Reflection: How have you been high-maintenance today? Call five people right now and ask their opinion. In what ways can you become more centered on self?

Habit #25

View People as Converts

*E*VEN A CASUAL Christian takes the Great Commission seriously. However, you can thwart any good intentions you have in this realm by treating people simply as potential converts.

The worst possible thing you can do in evangelism is to think of people as individuals, made in the image of God, loved by their Creator. Do not think of them as people for whom Christ died. Think of them as notches on your religious revolver.

You must cultivate a cavalier attitude toward the whole idea of "sharing your faith," and as much as possible take out the relational aspect of the task. Try to see non-Christians as a nameless, faceless mass of humanity rather than that neighbor down the street or your close relative.

Stick tracts in hotel rooms and drive-thrus, in phone booths and on windshields. Wear T-shirts that dramatically state the Christian message in a slogan, particularly if it's a rip-off of a secular advertisement. Do this not to get the message out, but to assuage your own feelings of guilt.

Mind you, there are some vibrant Christians who use tracts, T-shirts and other means to strike up conversations with unbelievers. But you must use these methods only as means to escape relationships.

Remember, the goal of evangelism for the ineffective Christian is not to bring others into the kingdom and a right relationship with God; it is to make you think you've done your duty, and ultimately to make you feel better.

For Further Thought: Think of one person who isn't a

Christian you could be praying for right now. Now stop thinking about that or you won't be ineffective.

Habit #26

Evangelize
Stellar Candidates

*T*HERE IS ONE exception to ineffective evangelism that should be addressed here. When you treat people like numbers, you will feel righteous for spreading the Word. To enhance this feeling you should utilize the "Stellar Candidate" approach.

Have you ever seen someone on television or in a film and wondered what it would be like if that person were to become a Christian? This is a perfectly natural thing for a believer to do, but you must take this thought to its extreme.

You must begin not only praying for the salvation of your stellar candidate—let's say the artist formerly known as "Billy-Bob"—but also writing the candidate and telling that person how much you are praying for him. Stalk Billy-Bob and convince yourself you're doing so out of Christian compassion.

Then begin telling others how much you are praying and writing Billy-Bob and how great the kingdom of God would be if only Billy-Bob would become a Christian! In this way you will plant in other minds the thought that is already full grown in your own, that God uses people with great talent and visibility in greater ways than he can ordinary, everyday people like yourself.

But by earnestly striving for the salvation of Billy-Bob, whose name you drop every few minutes, you elevate yourself above the ordinary and eventually will become known as "The Person Whose Ministry Is Praying for Billy-Bob."

Action Point: What singer, actor, politician, writer, news anchor, media mogul or billionaire would you like to be known as praying for? How much more would you pray for a celebrity than for a coworker?

Habit #27

Money Isn't Any of God's Business

*C*HRISTIANS WHO take their faith seriously know that finances are an integral part of their spiritual lives. How they use their money is a barometer of their trust in the provision of the Almighty.

But you, if you are to increase your ineffectiveness, should treat money as none of God's business. After all, it's yours, not his. You earned it, right? You should be able to spend it any way you please.

You will be tempted through onslaughts of Scriptures and Christian financial counselors to give to your church, to ministries that help you and to a variety of worthy causes. Treat these people like phone solicitors.

I have heard many committed Christians ask, "Should I tithe on the gross or after taxes?" This is entirely the wrong question. The correct question is "Why should I give at all?"

Remind yourself that God owns the cattle on a thousand hills and the riches of heaven. Compare that with the measly amount you make and you'll keep every penny.

Remember, you are setting an example before your children every week when that offering plate passes. You are letting them know how much you value the things of God, how much you trust him and wish to give back to him. If you want them to be ineffective, say you love God but palm the ten-dollar bill as the plate passes.

Ineffective Financial Exercise: Total your gross earnings for this year. Estimate your taxes. Total all your expenses. Divide the remainder by 10. Take that amount to the mall and treat yourself—you deserve it. If there's anything left over, think about giving it on Sunday.

Habit #28

Treat the Old Testament as a Storybook

ADAM. EVE. NOAH. Abraham. Moses. Joshua. Ruth. David. Solomon.

If you are to be ineffective as a Christian, you must treat these people as mere characters in God's little playhouse. Never, ever think of them as real humans who lived real lives.

Tell yourself it is not important whether someone like Esther actually lived in time and space. It is not important whether Abraham physically raised a knife to kill his son—I think it was Abraham, wasn't it?—or that Noah built a big boat and put all the animals on it.

What is important, you must convince yourself, is that these tales were passed from one generation to the next to emphasize a moral framework. Thus it's not important if there were really ten commandments written in stone (or that it was actual stone). The important thing is we have stories to tell children so they'll be good.

Tell yourself, and others, that because we have the New Testament it's not important to read anything before Matthew. It's not important to see the parallels between Israel and the church. It's not important to learn of the archaeological finds that match with the words of Old Testament writers.

In this way you will divorce history from the written text and, in the end, the truth spoken of in the Scriptures. Keep distance between yourself and the characters of the Old Testament, because you may see in them pictures of yourself and your own life that you don't want to see.

A Moment to Mull: What is your favorite Old Testament character? What actor/actress would you choose to play him/her in a movie of the week? Which director other than Oliver Stone would you choose?

Habit #29

Measure Success by Numbers

*I*F SOMEONE ASKS A business executive their definition of success, the professional would no doubt point to the bottom line. How much money was made in the previous year? A farmer will point to the number of bushels of corn or head of cattle.

For you, an ineffective Christian, what is the definition of success? The answer should be numbers. The more numbers of the nameless hordes you can attract to your church, Sunday school, conference or Bible study, the more success you possess.

This means you will do just about anything outside of breaking the Ten Commandments to get people in, and sometimes it's probably okay to do that.

Conversely, those who do not have numbers are not experiencing success. Look down on such people. Perhaps there is a small church struggling to make disciples, worship God and be faithful to its calling. Stay away from this type of place; it can only bring you closer to God.

Instead gravitate toward the large gatherings that attract numbers through artificial means. Of course there are larger ministries that seek to make disciples, worship and be faithful, and you should stay away from these as well.

With all that is in you, make numbers most important. Do not feel like you have done anything significant until you see lots of heads. Become discouraged and despair if you do not achieve the success you crave. This will thwart any real progress you may have made with those around you.

Ineffective Growth Exercise: What number would constitute success for church attendance? What number would constitute success for your yearly income? Write these two numbers down in a conspicuous place and refer to them often.

Habit #30
Blame Others

WHENEVER YOU are confronted with your sin, whenever you feel conviction in your spirit, whenever you are tempted to take responsibility for your actions, remember the ineffective Christian always blames others.

In the marriage relationship it is best when you are caught in the wrong to begin your next sentence with "I know that, but if you hadn't . . ." This shifts the blame for your actions back onto your spouse, which is a wonderful way to escape scrutiny.

When your coworkers discover a mistake you made at work, such as putting coffee grounds in the photocopier, blame someone else. Excuse yourself by saying, "I was confused. My last employer had a coffee machine bigger than this copier, and it made copies, received faxes and e-mails, and made cappuccino."

This is a particularly important element in the process of becoming an ineffective parent. When you make a mistake, expunge the guilt by placing blame and shame on the child rather than absorbing the fault yourself.

Finally, never, ever consider uttering the phrase "I'm wrong." Just as insurance companies urge you to never say it at the scene of an accident, you should never admit anything. Also, do not say "I'm sorry," or "Please forgive me."

When you blame others constantly for your mistakes, over time you will generate the belief that the only reason you sin is because of other people, or that you don't really sin at all. When you reach this point you are at the height of ineffectivity in your Christian life.

Bumper Sticker: Have you blamed your child today?

Habit #31

Leave Fasting to the Weird People

*I*F YOU WANT TO stay in a state of languor in your faith, shun the spiritual disciplines. Shrink from any activity that puts a degree of demand on your spirit, your intellect and your body.

For example, you must never fast. Fasting should be considered something weird people do. Think of fasting as an Old Testament phenomenon or something John the Baptist would do after a week of locust casserole.

Convince yourself that going without food for a period of time would be dangerous to your health or would set a bad example before your children. Think of any excuse plausible to give those around you.

Fasting points you toward the eternal and focuses you on things above. Fasting emphasizes that your body is subject to your will, that your appetite can be controlled. Those notions just don't fit with ineffective living.

If you find people who do fast regularly, run from them. They probably pray way too often and read their Bibles every day.

If you find that you are in a position where you must fast, make a big deal about it. Walk around with a long face and drool when you see someone munching on potato chips. Moan a lot. Every chance you get you should say something like "That sandwich really looks good, but I can't have any. Fasting, you know."

For Further Reflection: What foods would you least like to give up in a fast? Make a list and keep it handy when tempted to discipline your body.

Habit #32

Extinguish Hell

*H*ELL. DO YOU think about it much? Not if you're ineffective. Hell is a place that should never creep into your conscious thoughts if you desire to stay in the doldrums of faith.

If you really believed there was a place of eternal torment where friends and family members were headed if they did not know Christ, you would act much differently. You would take every opportunity to tell them about the forgiveness of God. You would pray and petition God for their souls. Nearly every waking moment would bring you before his throne to plead for them.

However, for ineffective Christians hell is a myth. It's meant to scare people, but it's not an actual place. Cultivate the vision of hell as pitchforks and horned devils. Make jokes about it. Laugh when others say, "That's where all the fun people are going." Do not become saddened over such statements.

Above all, you must not read what the Bible has to say about hell, particularly what Jesus said. A correct view of eternal separation from God, where the worm does not die, where there is weeping and gnashing of teeth, would cause you to shudder, cast yourself on the mercy of Almighty God and take your faith more seriously. If such thoughts do come into your mind, immediately think of something happy and tell yourself that God loves everyone and could never be so judgmental as to punish sinful people.

Scripture to Modify: Find words such as *perish, hell* and *torment* in your Bible and place a smiley face over them.

Habit #33

Christianity Is Religion, Not Relationship

*T*HE WAY YOU view your faith has a lot to do with the way you live; therefore you must never think of Christianity as a relationship with God, but as a religion.

A religion is a set of rules, a fixed system of tenets that make people think they are pleasing God. Some religions have stringent rules, while others are more relaxed. You may have to pray three times a day or fast at strategic points on the calendar. Or you might just have to pray before you eat every now and then. Thankfully, the Christian religion can be manipulated so that you don't have to do much at all, just say you believe.

Of course, if you treat your faith as a religion there will be times when you desire to act. There will no doubt be rules you decide to follow that simply make you feel "religious" and not at all like someone who doesn't go to church Sunday mornings.

Whatever your particular bent, never view your faith as a relationship. If you begin thinking about a personal God calling you to holiness and righteous living rather than a set of rules, you have taken a desperately wrong step.

Viewing God as wanting a relationship with you is an unfathomable thought in itself and will cause you to gaze at his glory in a new way. You will begin to want to please him rather than yourself. You will want to know his will instead of your own. Do not get caught in this vicious trap, or you will destroy all the ineffectiveness you have not worked so hard to attain.

Introspection Corner: Do you think God wants a relationship with you? Come on, really? Who do you think you are, anyway?

Habit #34

Approach God
Only to Get "Fixed"

*T*HERE ARE MANY ways to view God. Ineffective Christians approach him for one reason only: to get a holy "fix."

When you first come to him, you come not out of a sense of your sin and the overwhelming need of forgiveness, nor out of a response to the holiness of God, but because people around you look happy and you want what they have. You come because your wife is about to leave or the doctor has bad news or you're deep in consumer debt. You come to get fixed.

To be healed. For a makeover.

Of course effective Christians realize there is a great healing that comes from a relationship with God, but they view it not as a quick fix but as a healing of the soul. They see forgiveness of sin as an eternal issue that supersedes all the temporal needs of earth. Effective Christians serve God in spite of difficulty. You, however, must serve God as long as he meets your needs.

In a church setting this can provide wonderful opportunities to spread the mediocrity. In your evangelism, you can bring in droves of people by simply making the gospel a pill you take to get your needs met. In this view, saying yes to Jesus does not make him Lord, but the great server, the almighty dispenser of health and wealth and perfect smiles.

God is there for you, pal. Teach others this truth and you will sink to new depths of ineffectiveness.

For Further Thought: What need can God meet for you today? If God didn't meet your perceived needs, would you still want to be a Christian? How quickly would you like to be fixed?

Habit #35

Live Superstitiously

I CANNOT TELL YOU how many Christians I meet who have found new and creative ways to be ineffective. One I have observed recently is the superstitious Christian.

A superstitious believer is one who puts stock in circumstance and chance. This person believes every occurrence is a sign from the Almighty for whatever decision they're about to make.

If they're looking for a new boyfriend and meet some

handsome man whose name is Bill on a train ride into the city, they believe it must be from God because their father's name was Bill, their boss is named Bill, and they got a bill from the electric company that very morning. The fact that the Bill on the train is not a Christian does not concern the person; this is incidental. Bill's middle name is Wayne, and your niece says "waining" instead of "raining," so this is further cause to believe he is Mr. Right.

Other superstitious Christians look at Scripture and discover unique meanings and applications for specific verses. When a banker I know was deciding whether to deal underhandedly in a certain transaction, he read Philippians 2:4: "Each of you should look not only to your own interests, but also to the interests of others." He thought God was telling him to go ahead with the deal as long as he gave a percentage of the interest to the church.

Those who treat the Bible like a horoscope (and actually read their horoscope every day) will be all the more ineffective for it.

Superstitious Steps to Ineffectivity

Step 1. What important decision do you have to make today?

Step 2. What answer do you most want?

Step 3. Answer those questions, then open your Bible and find a passage that will confirm Step 2.

Habit #36

Live in the Future

*T*HERE ARE TWO tenses for the ineffective Christian to reside in. One is the future.

I do not mean by this that the person should consider

eternity and life in the hereafter. If a person were to do that, he or she would surely become more effective. I am talking about the future as in tomorrow and next week and next year.

When you were a child you longed to be older. You longed for the responsibility that older children had, then the opportunities teenagers and adults possessed. You did not take advantage of the current moment but lived looking forward to a time that never came. You were never content in the present. This is how you must live out your faith.

If you are in college, you must yearn for the time when you will be out. If you are single, you must yearn to be married. If you are in the midst of your work years, you must long for retirement. If you have small children, you should yearn for an empty nest.

By living in the future you do not take advantage of the present. You do not fully learn in college. You do not take advantage of your singleness or work for God's glory. You do not enjoy the kids' giggles and smiles while they are still around.

This future living could be called an "if only" life. If only I were done with this, I would be happy. Remember, live in the future and you will never truly live in the present.

Question to Ponder: What are you waiting for that's putting your life on hold? Hang on to it today much more tightly.

Habit #37

Live in the Past

*I*F AN INEFFECTIVE Christian is not living in the future, he or she should live in the past. This may be the best way to stay in a state of spiritual decline.

You must understand that many effective Christians use the

past for great good. They remember the sin of the past and ask forgiveness. They remember the lessons of the past and act on them. They seek change in themselves because of the past.

I do not want you to do such things. You should longingly desire the past. You must convince yourself it was always better "back then." The hymns were richer. The revivals lasted longer. The fellowship was sweeter. The potluck dinners were not low-fat. The people were more considerate. The missionaries stayed away longer. You didn't have to give as much in the offering to feel good about it.

Unlike the future, which eventually arrives and becomes the present, the past can never come again, so you must bring it back with your mind. Wallow in it. Suck the marrow from the past in your mind, and your eyes will be so glazed that you will not be able to perceive the gift God gives you in the present.

You must always look either backward or forward. Never stand in this moment, the now, and ask what God would have you do for his glory. Do not be content with the smile of a spouse, the purple-orange of the sunset or the feel of a child's hand slipping effortlessly into your own. The smiles, sunsets and hands were always better in the past.

Wise Saying: Constantly compare the past with the present and you will escape any responsibility to change the future.

Habit #38

Do Not View Your Body as God's Temple

*O*F ALL THE WAYS TO be ineffective in your Christian life, this habit may be the easiest to master. You must view your body as your own and not God's temple. You may achieve this in a variety of ways.

First, excessive food intake. One of the hallmarks for sub-par Christians is to always want more. This works wonderfully in the area of diet, since you have a daily need of sustenance. God has created in you a natural hunger. The ineffective Christian will take this need and turn it into gluttony. A steak here, a piece of pie there, a Little Debbie Oatmeal Cream Pie (or Star Crunch) on the side, and pretty soon you resemble the *Hindenburg.*

You can also mar God's plan for food by taking too little. Spurning God's little pleasures of fruits and delicacies not only will make you thin but will cause you to feel you are much more spiritual than others. Food intake can lead to gluttony or pride, which are both conduits to ineffectivity.

Since you think about spiritual things at select times, resist the urge to view your body as the lodging place for the Holy Spirit. If for one minute you truly believed that God was making his dwelling inside you, what you eat, what you watch on television, how much time you spend reading the Bible and how you treat your neighbor would all change. Don't view your body as the temple of God; see it as your home, your castle, your private pleasure palace. Eat, drink and be merry! Or starve yourself. It's your party.

Scripture to Avoid: 1 Corinthians 6:19-20

Habit #39

Cultivate Prejudice

AS A FAMOUS ineffective Christian once said—I think it was me—"Judge people by the color of their skin, the language they speak, the clothes they can afford and the way they look, not on the content of their character."

Every day you must cultivate prejudice in your life if you are to live down to my standards. You must set yourself above others in any way possible to show you are superior. Cultivate prejudice by looking down on anyone who is different from you. Skin color, weight, ethnic background, mixed race, height, shoe size or eye color—any of these standards will do.

Caricature people from different parts of the country. Think of snappy things to say about those lazy people from the South, those stupid people from the North, those snobby people from the East or those crazy people out West.

Categorize others. In your mind make certain categories of behavior for people you think are different. This way you will not have to deal with individuals but can, at a glance, judge the motives and intent of anyone on the planet.

Above all, you must not get to know anyone who is different from you, for this would break down stereotypes and cause you to treat others as equals, with respect and with dignity.

Questions to Ponder: Do you have a good friend who is Caucasian? Do you have a good friend who is African-American? Do you have a good friend who is Hispanic? Do you have a good friend who is Native American? If you answered yes to more than one of the above, it is time for you to move.

Habit #40

Shun Joy

*E*VERY DAY YOU choose a way to look at life. Nothing robs you of your ineffectiveness like joy. You must shun it.

Shun joy in the morning when you wake up and notice you have another chance at life. Shun joy when you see the sun rise in splendor. Do not let this sight make you think of the pure light of heaven that is Christ.

Shun joy with your children, particularly when they are small. Notice the diapers, the cuts and scrapes, the whining, crying milieu. Do not for a moment thank God for loaning you these little lives to mold and shape. Do not pick up your child and hold her in your arms for the express purpose of enjoying her. Pick a child up only when you are about to discipline her.

Shun joy as you go about your work. Do not revel in the gifts and talents given you or thank God you can use them to help others.

Shun joy in music. If a particular style makes you light-hearted and desirous of skipping or dancing about the kitchen, tell yourself this is sinful and should not be done by sober-minded people.

Stop smiling, for this is an expression of joy. Squelch any feeling deep within that wants to spring forth in thanksgiving and praise. When you have accomplished the above in your own life, you must spread the feeling to others, which will happen naturally if you follow these directives.

Action Point: Eat a dill pickle and a freshly cut lemon. Immediately look in the mirror. This is how you should appear at all times.

Habit #41

Don't Believe Jesus Is the Only Way to God

SINCE THERE ARE many sincere people in the world who want to be good and work their way to God, you must *not* believe that Jesus is the only way to heaven.

Like the doctrine of hell, belief in the exclusivity of salvation through Jesus is a great motivator for Christians. It compels them to share their faith and spread the word of Christ's claim to lordship.

But you must look at this concept rationally and convince yourself that you are being loving and wise to believe that Jesus isn't the only way. After all, what kind of God would force people to believe something they haven't heard or don't like? That would be cruel, wouldn't it?

Therefore you should foster the belief that all you need is sincerity in your faith. The object of that faith does not matter. It could be Buddha, Muhammad, a stone or a dead ancestor. This chips away at the possibility of absolute truth and the fact that God has the right to make the rules no matter what you think. Further, it puts you in the place of God, which is just where an ineffective Christian should be.

Do not concern yourself with the fields white unto harvest, for if sincerity is the key to faith they don't really need your help. They can find their own way. Just be happy that you have a belief in Jesus and go about your business as usual.

Scripture to Avoid: Acts 4:10-12

Habit #42

Take Grace for Granted

*O*NE OF THE GREAT theological truths of Christianity is encompassed in the word *grace*. To have as little effect as possible on those around you, take grace for granted.

You do this by pointing to an aisle you walked long ago as the reference point for your faith. When you are asked, "How do you know you are a Christian?" you should answer, "Because when

I was five, I gave up my life of wanton sin and went forward."

Do not consider the fact that God's working in your life today is as much an evidence of his grace as the time you toddled down the aisle in your knickers. If perhaps you do not sense God working, if you do not see a change in behavior and in attitude today, the walk you took as a child may not have meant much and this may be the reason for your ineffectiveness. But you must not think about this; rather continue in this state.

Take grace for granted by sinning and sinning and sinning. When you are convicted about a certain action or pattern of behavior, tilt your head, shrug your shoulders and say, "It's been paid for, no big wup." Live as if God's grace covers every sin with no consequences, and live your ungodliness overtly.

Take grace for granted by condemning others. Never let the words "There but for the grace of God go I" enter your consciousness. A condemning spirit tramples God's grace like an unwanted bug.

Thought for the Day: When you see some unfortunate person, repeat to yourself this phrase: *Boy, I sure am glad I'm better than they are!*

Habit #43

Believe Sex Is Dirty

ANOTHER WAY TO cultivate ineffective Christian living is to take what God has given as a gift and pervert it or treat it wrongly. This can be achieved with anchovies (on pizza), with blue cheese dressing (on a salad) and especially with sex.

It would be easy for me to encourage you toward sexual promiscuity and debauchery. However, I suggest you treat sex as something inherently nasty, vile, filthy, animal-like and disgusting. This will frustrate your mate to no end and communicate that intimacy is not carried out with the whole person, just the mind. It will also start you on the slippery slope of twisting God's goodness into something unseemly.

If you look at sex between husband and wife as a grotesque, writhing maelstrom, you will miss the opportunity of creatively expressing love to your mate in a physical manner. And if you can take away this expression, pretty soon you can justify the end of any tangible demonstration of love and intimacy.

Confirm your opinion by pointing to all the problems sex wrought in Old Testament days. Then show the negative ways our culture misuses sex to sell products and entice people toward lust, lasciviousness and network miniseries. If this argument held water, of course, you wouldn't be able to breathe.

Remember, the father of lies has twisted all good things provided by the Father of Lights. Believe sex is dirty and treat this gift as a curse.

Scripture to Avoid: The Song of Solomon

Habit #44

Believe You Must Tidy Up Before Coming to God

*T*HE WAY GOD views humans is, of course, drastically opposed to the way you should view them if you are to be ineffective. But it is also important to view God in certain ineffective ways. Primarily you need to believe that to approach him, you must be cleaned up. Tidy. Presentable. In order for people to have a relationship with this eternal being, they must get their life in order and *then* pray to him/join a church/sing in the choir.

This mindset will accomplish two things. First, for those who have a particularly sensitive conscience, it will keep them from ever coming to God. They view themselves as utterly sinful the moment they eat the last Chiclet in the box. If they believe they must be tidy in order to have a relationship with God, they will never enter into it, because deep down they know their hearts are wicked.

Second, this mindset causes a false sense of pride in your own holiness. You come to God not recognizing your sin, but feeling that you have pulled yourself up by your spiritual bootstraps and now deserve the favor of the Almighty.

Feeling you must be tidy to come to God will keep you at a distance from him, which is your goal. When you get the urge to get more involved in church activities, think about how much better everyone else is and wait until you can "get it together." This will not only keep you from growing but also rob your fellow Christians of a nice voice in the choir, helping hands at the homeless shelter or an usher with a firm handshake instead of a dead fish.

For Further Thought: How much work would you have to do to become "tidy" before God today?

Habit #45

Don't Be Real
with God

*I*N MY SURVEYS OF mediocre Christians, I have noticed a common trait. Nearly 100 percent of them avoid any sense of reality with God. I urge you to duplicate their actions.

Make sure the few moments you devote to prayer during the week do not include expressions from the depths of your being. Do not bring God your disappointments or struggles. Do not tell him how frustrated you are about your gene pool, your high mortgage or the fact that the tip of your cane keeps falling off. Make things nice and pleasant. Deny, deny, deny, particularly if your frustration is really with God.

This again keeps God at a distance from your life and does not acknowledge your true feelings. If you were to hash those things out with your heavenly Father, chances are you would have a quite different view of them when you completed your prayer.

Keeping your deep thoughts and emotions from God also makes you believe that he doesn't already know what is in the depth of your soul. It reinforces the false perception that you can hide things from God. You begin to believe hiding things from him is actually a virtue for those who want to be "spiritual."

Remember the old saying "Never let them see you sweat"? Apply this to God. Never let him see you be real. Practice the same type of dual living you exhibit before your family and friends, thinking and feeling one thing but acting in a totally different way. As you look in the rear-view mirror of life, you'll see your faith become smaller than it actually appears.

Scriptures to Avoid: The Psalms

Habit #46
Believe God's Will
Is Elusive & Oppressive

As I HAVE SAID, the way you view God is quite important for how much you grow in your Christian life. Therefore, to stay as stagnant as possible, you must see God's will as both elusive and oppressive.

Always pine for direct knowledge from God about any choices you may face. When you do not hear an audible voice from the clouds, this means God is stingy and enjoys playing a celestial game of hide-and-seek with his will. Never mind that he has given you a brain, his Word and the Holy Spirit. You must constantly focus on the fact that he has not stepped out of heaven to tell you whether or not to buy or build a new house.

On the other hand, you should always believe God's will is oppressive in nature. If he did step out of the clouds and give you direct instructions for the details of your life, you must believe he would only give you things that do not satisfy. He will send you to Africa. He will make you single the rest of your life. He will kink your Slinky. Looking at the short-term effects, the temporal rather than the eternal, will help you believe that his will is inherently bad.

Of course, it just may be that God's will for you is where you are right now. He just might be trying to teach you through your present situation. Therefore it is imperative to keep looking elsewhere, believing God is both stingy and mean in his dealings with you.

Scripture to Avoid: Psalm 37:4-5

Habit #47

Avoid Unity in the Body

*I*NEFFECTIVE CHRISTIANS stay to themselves. They do not congregate with others who have the slightest difference in theology or practice. If you truly desire a terminal spiritual life, you will avoid unity at all costs.

If you do not raise your hands in worship, shun those who do.

If you dunk, stay away from the sprinklers. If there is a disaster in the community or a worthy cause that could unite people across denominational lines, do not join hands in Christian love, for this would only make the world look on in wonder.

If you should be challenged to associate with someone of another church background, resist the temptation by caricaturing others' beliefs: "You know what those Baptists believe," or "Those Presbyterians think they're better than anybody else," or "Methodists don't like banjos." Concentrate on dogma, not people.

Do not for a moment believe any song that encourages unity. Ineffective Christians believe that in Christ there is East, West, North, South and Middle. They sing, "And they'll know we are Christians by how far apart we are."

If you find disunity unappealing, promulgate the other extreme of false unity. Accept anyone who says they are Christian no matter what they believe about the person of Christ. Warmly welcome those who think Jesus was "simply a good teacher" or "just another of the great prophets." These people may not have their theology down, but they're sincere and really nice.

Remember, you have two options: (1) never accept any shade of theological difference within your fellowship, or (2) water down your congregation with spurious believers. Either extreme will keep you ineffective in your Christian life.

Scriptures to Avoid: Ephesians 4:3; John 17:21

Habit #48

Live like a Chameleon

*A*UTHENTICITY, balance and consistency are marks of the Christian. You should oppose these characteristics with every fiber of your being and live like a chameleon.

A chameleon changes color whenever its surroundings change, and you must as well. When it is Sunday and you are in church, you should smile and present the appearance that you are a spiritual person. But when you reach the water cooler Monday morning, laugh at the off-color jokes and throw in a few barbs at minorities for good measure.

Among racists, you must also be racist. Among gossips, gossip. Among sports fanatics, throw out statistics and memorable plays with the best of them. Among drinkers, drink. Among teetotalers, abstain. In other words, when with pagans, act like a pagan, when with Christians, act like a Christian.

If you begin feeling a slight bit of guilt for your actions, convince yourself that you're living up to the biblical ideal of being all things to all people, when in actuality you're being nothing to anyone but a big fake.

The ineffective Christian believes the most important aspect of life is appearance, so change the way you look and act when you are around people with different values, different priorities and beliefs. The more your life reflects the actions of a chameleon, the more ineffective you will become.

Action Point: Record a phone conversation with a friend from church and a friend from the bowling league. What words were different? How many references to God were made in both?

Habit #49

Be Impatient

*I*MPATIENCE IS the second cousin to worry, which is another trait of faithless living. You must pick and prune impatience from day to day and learn how to make every aspect of your life controlled by your own desires.

Be impatient with things. Honk in traffic and run your hands through your hair at every red light. When you are assembling Christmas toys, fixing household appliances, making dinner or waiting for the mail to come, be impatient. Huff about the house because things won't cooperate with your agenda.

Be impatient with people. When someone does not live up to the standards you set, demand that they change. At the grocery store, tap your foot and expel air when the cashier does not ring your food up in record time. Make snide comments about the laziness of toll-booth operators. Scold children for not reaching the car and buckling their seat belts when you're ready to pull out. Snap at your auto mechanic for his lack of attention to your timing chain.

Finally, be impatient with God. Nothing can possibly make you more ineffective than setting demands the Almighty must meet. Keep him apprised of *your* timetable and *your* plans. When he doesn't meet those expectations, take hold of the situation and act quickly.

Under no circumstances should you wait for God to act. Waiting proves you truly trust in God and not yourself.

Scripture to Avoid: Isaiah 40:31

Habit #50

Have All the Answers

NO MATTER WHAT kind of life you lead, you will no doubt come in contact with people who are experiencing troubles and trials. And when people question their faith, it is imperative that you have all the answers.

I do not mean that you should understand the biblical view of suffering. I do not mean you should discern the bedrock theological questions of sincere people. That would be dangerous. I mean you should cultivate an attitude that you have figured out life. You know every question and have snappy answers to boot. Communicate to others that there are no mysteries left to plumb, because you have it all down.

Never just sit and mourn with a friend; say something. Never identify with someone who is struggling. Never simply weep and admit you have felt the same feelings. Give verses, even out of context if you have to. Give short pithy sayings like "This too shall pass." If you can quickly silence a question with a sentence, you have done a great thing, particularly if you can make it rhyme.

You must also take on yourself the weight of the person's problems and believe if you don't have the answers he or she will fall away. If you don't fix the person right then and there, he or she will be lost forever. In this you promote the idea that God is not sovereign, *you* are. He does not control the destiny of the soul and the universe, *you* do. This is why you must act as if you have all the answers.

Action Point: Write out all the answers you have and keep them handy. When trouble comes, you'll need them.

Habit #51

Become a Walking Cliché

*T*HE INEFFECTIVE Christian not only has all the answers but maximizes his or her points by using clichés.

For example, when you meet someone who has just lost a loved one to a natural disaster, glibly state, "All things work together for good!" Smile knowingly as you repeat this phrase over and over. This demonstrates the awesome hold cliché has on truth.

When a parent agonizes over a child who has gone away to college, shake your head and say, "You really need to let go and let God." This intensifies the pain the person already feels and may cause them to stuff their emotions around those who could truly empathize.

"God said it, I believe it, that settles it!" is a great slogan to use around intellectuals. If someone has made a life study in the sciences, it would be good to caricature their data by saying, "He believes my nearest relative is down at the zoo." Never give an honest ear to a finding that seems to conflict with Scripture. This makes you close-minded and narrow, which is exactly the kind of life an ineffective Christian leads.

Don't just say the clichés, wear them boldly on T-shirts and jackets. Send them on your checks, plaster them on your car, illuminate them during the holidays, and always remember the proverb "A word fitly spoken can be turned into a cliché if you really work at it."

Cliché to Memorize: Jesus is the reason for the season.

Habit #52

Walk by Sight,
Not by Faith

*C*HRISTIANS WHO are rooted in the Bible know God desires a life lived by faith, a total surrender of the will and a casting of oneself on God's mercy. However, if you want to be spiritually ineffective you will walk by sight, not by faith.

Walking by sight means you do not act on the truth revealed in the Scriptures; rather you seek a sign or outward rendering of God to follow. (Such as Gideon's fleece in the Old Testament or, in modern times, Dr. Lacking's electric blanket. I would like to add a word of caution about testing God in this way, because we nearly lost the dear fellow.)

Walking by sight will cause you to follow God only when you feel he is leading you. In the night, when you are alone, filled with doubt and fear for the future, you should not reflect on God's faithfulness in the past. You should not cast your eyes on the word and realize how much the Father cares for you. Instead lean on your own understanding. Judge God by what you can see happening around you.

Walk by sight in the big decisions of life. Walk by sight in the small ones. Do not put any of your hope in things that cannot be seen, such as heaven, and you will live a gloriously ineffective Christian life.

Ineffective Reminder: Always unplug your fleece.

Habit #53

Be a Spiritual Weenie

*T*HE BIBLE AND church history are filled with accounts of men and women who stood up for their beliefs and their God. However, the ineffective Christian will learn the plethora of ways he or she can become a spiritual weenie.

Remember, becoming a weenie is a choice. A process. First you must convince yourself that restraint is the better part of valor. If you find yourself in a situation where you think it might be good to speak up or act on a spiritual matter, hold back because you want others to see how truly winsome you are.

If an unbeliever who has no idea of your religiosity takes a few jabs at the church, the Bible and God, do not be prepared with a reasoned answer. You must keep the hope that is within you bottled up for fear that someone might begin attacking you.

Perhaps you will find yourself among church people who begin gossiping and slandering someone in the fold. At this point you must never rebuke them, for it might make their self-esteem plunge. Instead laugh, nod your head and join in the skewering of your fellow believer.

As you progress through various levels of weenieness, you will find it easier to live a limp faith. You will look throughout the centuries at people who have been jailed, mocked, scorned and even killed for their belief in God. You will not want to become a statistic. As much as possible keep your faith to yourself and your head on your shoulders. As someone wise once said, look out for number one.

Scripture to Avoid: 1 Peter 3:15

Habit #54

Believe Spiritual Warfare Is Fiction

*E*VERYONE KNOWS how much fun Frank Peretti has had with angels and demons warring in the heavenlies. If you are to live ineffectively as a Christian, you must never believe there is such a thing as a spiritual battle.

Angels are meant to be trinkets you hang on Christmas trees. They are ornaments for festive people. They are fads, showing up in secular and sacred books and calendars. Interest in angels should be encouraged as long as the truth about them is never explored. Angels are playthings, not reality.

Conversely, demons should be considered the "dark side" of the playground, the yang to the yin. Demons are needed to balance out the stories told around the spiritual campfire, the villains of our tales of faith.

Under no circumstances should you read the Old Testament, which assumes the reality of angels. Under no circumstances should you read any prophetic literature like Revelation. However, if you do happen onto any of these passages, convince yourself that angels are simply metaphors of God's light and goodness.

If you were to take the spiritual battle seriously and the fight that is going on for the souls of humanity, you would no doubt pray more, seek to live a holier life and strive to tell others the good news. You would see heavenly angels as your ally in this fight and fallen angels as part of the enemy's dastardly plan. You would take on the weapons of warfare and wade into the battle.

Don't do this. Spiritual warfare is fiction.
Scripture to Avoid: Ephesians 6:12

Habit #55

Judge Others

*I*NEFFECTIVE Christians have a tendency to look past their own sin. This is very good. One of the best ways to continue in this state is to look at others in a spirit of judgment.

Judge others' actions. When you see the child of a friend do a bit of mischief, judge the parents for their lack of discipline in the home.

Judge others' words. Be so picky about grammar that people are afraid to speak around you. If a subject and a verb disagree, stop others in midsentence to correct them. Judge accents. Judge the choice of words, saying, "You don't mean *vital,* you mean *integral.* There's a difference." This puts you above others and makes you feel superior. However, you should judge unkind words only when they are spoken about you.

Judge others' motives. Cultivate the uncanny ability to get into the minds of others so that you know exactly what they are thinking and why they do certain things. It is imperative that you relate these truths to friends: "The pastor preached that sermon because he struggles with that sin," or, "The elders want a gymnasium built so they can put their names on the front of the building."

Do not show grace to others. Do not give the benefit of the doubt. Never take someone at face value for what they say or do. And when someone says, "Judge not, lest ye be judged," believe their motives are impure as well.

Thought to Ponder: If others judged you the way you judge

others, how would your church be different? Would we need altars or gallows?

Habit #56

Overanalyze Every Situation

*P*OP PSYCHOLOGY has provided a number of wonderful conduits for ineffectivity. Overanalyzing a situation rather than calling it sin is one of the best. I urge you to sit down with a good self-help book and begin today.

It is important that you emphasize self-esteem. "I'm only acting this way because my self-esteem is low." You can use this excuse for everything from an outburst of anger to murder. It may be true that your self-esteem is low, but you must exploit the term for maximum effect.

Overanalyze others, and it will either drive them crazy or wear them down to the point where they eventually agree with your assessment. "You're obese not because of these empty potato-chip bags, but because of the way the mailman used to deliver postcards to you when you were a child."

Overanalyzing may serve you best when there's nothing wrong and no sin has been committed, but because of your keen senses others begin to believe there's something wrong. "The pastor's wife wore that dress because she secretly resents the congregation," or, "You don't like my chicken casserole because your inner child abhors poultry." When someone at church doesn't greet you in just the right way, judge them. Believe the worst, that they suddenly hate you and want to do terrible things to your pets while you're away on vacation.

The key is always looking at the psychological, not the

spiritual, component of people's actions. Remember, you will be most ineffective when you overanalyze others.

Action Point: Overanalyze why you are reading this book. What is the deep, dark secret that caused you to choose it? You want to buy another, don't you?

Habit #57

Scare or Skirt When Talking About God

*L*ET ME POSE TWO conversation scenarios you should set up while sitting beside strangers. Many Christians feel guilty for not sharing the gospel more often in these situations, but as an ineffective believer, you must seize the moment to be as ineffective as possible.

The scene is an airport terminal. You are on a business trip for your company.

PERSON 1:	Are you heading to Portland on business?
YOU:	Yes.
PERSON 1:	It's supposed to be nice there today.
YOU:	Good.
PERSON 1:	I see you carry a Bible in your briefcase. Why?
YOU:	I don't know. Maybe my wife stuck it in there.
PERSON 1:	So, are you one of those Christians?
YOU:	Look, can't a guy carry a Bible without being interrogated? It's not against the law, you know.

This is "the skirt." Whenever an opportunity arises to speak about God, you must do an end run around the conversation. Make the other person feel guilty for bringing it up.

The other extreme works nicely as well. It is called "the scare."

PERSON 2:   Are you heading to Portland on business?

YOU: Yes, the Lord has called me to Portland. He talks to me, you know.

PERSON 2:   Really? Well, uh . . . it's supposed to be nice there today.

YOU: Well, praise God! Would you like to pray and become a Christian right now?

PERSON 2:   Uh, I think I have to change flights, excuse me.

Action Point: Find someone today at a bus stop, on an airplane or in an elevator and use one of the above.

Habit #58

Live a Safe Life

YOU HAVE HEARD it said that the Christian life is a great adventure. You have heard it said that the world has not seen what God can do through a person totally surrendered to him. But you may not have heard that the ineffective life is the safe life.

Do not take chances with your existence. Do not consider going to places where there is persecution and where people have been known to criticize Christians. You certainly should never consider living where Christians are mocked, scorned and even killed. This could seriously hamper your golf game.

You really need to keep yourself safe financially. If you're thinking about Christian service of some kind, do not jump into things. Take a few years. Make a little money. Get a nest egg saved up and then decide if you want to do something foolish.

Keep yourself safe physically by buying a home in the suburbs or in a rural area. Do not live in the inner city where crime and poverty reign. Build walls between your congregation and your community. Do not try to minister to people who have serious diseases. Leave that to little women from Calcutta who don't have the sense to come in out of the slums.

Keep yourself safe spiritually by avoiding any direct contact with the enemy of your soul. If you sense antagonism or some kind of spiritual warfare, withdraw immediately. You may put yourself in danger. Remember, self-preservation is the most important thing for the ineffective believer.

Introspection Corner: In what ways can I shrink from stepping out in faith and make my life less of an adventure?

Habit #59

Embrace the Triangle of Mediocrity

*T*HERE ARE MANY ways to look at the ineffective life, and since most ineffective people are visual, I present the Triangle of Mediocrity.

At the bottom right corner of the triangle you see your natural abilities. These are the things you do in your own strength. These are talents and bents you have. Your triangle should lean heavily toward this end.

In the bottom left is "spiritual gifts." If you are ineffective, you probably are oblivious to your spiritual gifts. Do not try to discover them. You can only harm yourself if you acknowledge God's intervention in your life.

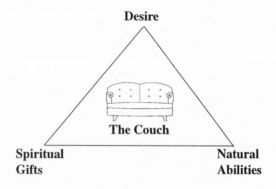

Figure 2

At the top of the triangle is your desire. This represents what drives your life. In the spiritually minded person, desire fuels gifts and abilities. In you, desire should be focused on self or the middle of the triangle, the couch.

Action Point: Analyze your life in relation to the triangle of mediocrity. In what ways must you change to become more unbalanced?

Habit #60

Put Your Faith in One Person

SINCE IT IS very difficult to follow a God you cannot see or feel or hear, one habit that invariably leads to ineffective Christianity is to place your faith in a person.

This may be a pastor or teacher in your church, but it might be better to choose some well-known author, speaker or celebrity. These are people you only see from a distance. You have no ability for a close relationship with them, so it's easier to put them on a pedestal.

You must idolize this person. Quote the person in daily conversation. Say things like "You know what [IDOL] says about that, don't you?" Buy autographed copies of your idol's books. Place this individual on the same par with the apostles and prophets, and follow even the most inane statements made by the person.

Instead of studying the Bible yourself, follow your idol's particular theological bent. Do not dig into particularly difficult passages; turn to your "authority." In this way you put the person in the place of God, and anyone put in God's place will eventually let you down.

When the person you idolize is exposed as a human being in all his or her frailty, you must be shocked senseless. Drown in self-pity and continue your spiritual depression for days. Be tempted to lose your faith, and tell others that God has let you down, when in reality it wasn't God you were trusting in the first place.

Action Point: Write a letter to a famous Christian today and ask for a handkerchief or worn sock to keep with you always.

Habit #61

Speak Christianese

As you can tell from this book, hiding your faith "under a bushel" is one great way to remain mediocre. There is another way to douse the light of faith and still verbalize your belief in Christianity. This use of language will marginalize your message and make you incomprehensible to the watching world. Whenever you are afforded the opportunity, speak "Christianese."

Christianese is that rare language of those in the "in" club. If you learn to master its usage, you will feel like you're part of the inner circle of the righteous, whether you are or not. It's easy to mistake the real thing for a counterfeit when listening to Christianese.

A few favorite phrases of the language are

□ born again
□ a real blessing in my life
□ asked Jesus into my heart
□ let me share this with you
□ what a time of fellowship we had
□ Jesus is my *personal* Savior
□ the Spirit really spoke to me

These phrases are harmless in themselves, but when used liberally they become a cacophony of spiritual goo. Do not seek to communicate truth to your audience, do not seek to understand the message yourself, seek only to know the holy lingo and spread it around.

Being able to speak this language will eventually cause you to take for granted the things you are saying. You will become so proficient in speaking Christianese that it will simply roll off the tongue like an aimless salvo at the firing range.

Action Point: Write your testimony using Christianese so your message will be incomprehensible to anyone but you. It will really be a blessing to your heart.

Habit #62

Practice Spiritual Procrastination

I PUT OFF WRITING this chapter for quite some time. In the grand scheme of ineffective living, this discipline is better than failing to finish a task.

Spiritual procrastination is the process by which you convince yourself you are aiming high while actually achieving nothing. Spiritual procrastination seems on the surface to vault you to a deeper level of faith, but in reality it keeps you mired in the sludge of mediocrity.

For example, let's say you desire to read through the Bible in one year. It's a commendable goal and makes you look good. Since January is the month for beginnings, search diligently for just the right translation with just the right study notes. Consult friends, pastors and bookstore owners. In two or three months you will have no excuse not to go out and buy it, but you must shop around for the best price. Like its secular counterpart, spiritual procrastination will not allow you to act on anything unless you've taken enough time to feel really guilty about it.

When you hear yourself saying, "You know, I really need to just get moving on buying this Bible," it will be summer. And since you simply can't start something as big as reading through the entire Bible during any month but January, you take at least six months to get prepared and spread the word around.

The motto of a spiritual procrastinator is always "Why not put off till tomorrow what you could easily do today?" Follow this and you will reach new lows of Christian complacency.

Question to Ponder: What spiritual effort can I put off today that will enhance my ineffectivity?

Habit #63

Believe New Is Always Better

*T*HERE IS A great treasure available to you in the history of the church. Therefore I urge you, ineffective ones, that you reject anything that's been around more than ten years.

Stay away from great hymns. Never study the words to "Amazing Grace," for you may see how much a wretch you really are. Never sing "Holy, Holy, Holy," for you may catch a glimpse of the purity and splendor of the Almighty.

Because those around you may not know what a "royal diadem" is, shun "All Hail the Power of Jesus' Name." Some may be offended that God is described as having "chariots of wrath," so stay away from "O Worship the King." Others will no doubt protest the military nature of "A Mighty Fortress," so do not let this hymn be included in your repertoire.

Do not stop at music, however. You must shun things such as the Apostles' Creed. Denigrate the sermons of Spurgeon, the writings of Chambers and books without a market niche. By doing so, you separate yourself from those who have written and voiced their faith throughout the ages. You make their contribution to the faith and succeeding generations patently nil, and raise the standard of contemporaneity as the most important.

If you cannot plow these songs and texts under the soil of church history, change their words to make them seem new, which is something like changing the nose on the *Mona Lisa*.

Action Point: Rewrite the text to "I Know Whom I Have Believed," changing the title to "Hey, I'm Happy Today!"

Habit #64

Rush to Easter & Skip Good Friday

*G*OOD FRIDAY IS one of those holidays you should just let slip by without much fanfare. Of course you should let your children get into the eggs and the bunnies and pretty outfits that cloud Easter fairly well, but I find that those who are ineffective treat Good Friday with a blasé attitude.

Good Friday isn't as easy to celebrate as Easter or Christmas. You don't say, "Merry Good Friday!" to people passing. You don't have a warm, fuzzy crèche and a baby to catch your attention. You have spikes driven in flesh, a crown of thorns on a pure head, and a crude, splinter-laden cross.

Good Friday reminds you of the suffering Christ endured for your sin. Good Friday shows you the extent to which God would go to redeem your soul. One thought of the punishment of Jesus on the cross, and half the things you do during the day would be reevaluated.

Therefore, you must not think about it much. Rush to Easter. Do not dwell on the crucifixion. Do not linger on the passion of Christ, his blood spilled for you, his hands and side pierced. Run to the empty tomb first. Dodge the scenes of agony. Skirting Good Friday makes your holiday much more positive. People will feel less sensitive over the price God paid to obtain their salvation.

Ineffective Exercise: To better celebrate the meaning of the day, use Good Friday to get things done around the house.

Habit #65

Marginalize Christmas

*T*HIS ONE SEEMS so obvious, but it remains one of the best ways to keep Christians from focusing on the truth of Christianity. In your preparation for the holiday, you must marginalize the real message of Christmas.

First, marginalize Christmas to your non-Christian friends. This can be as simple as saying the cliché you learned in Habit #51, "Jesus is the reason for the season!" Say it again and again. Or go to the other extreme and say nothing about the real meaning behind the holiday. Let your Christian ornaments do the talking. Whichever method you find most ineffective, choose and use it.

Marginalize Christmas to society. Make them think that your one mission in life is to get the crèche on the courthouse lawn, rather than to communicate the truth of Christ. Bring lawsuits, congregate angry mobs, and demand your right to free speech rather than speaking winsomely about the Savior.

Marginalize Christmas in your life. It is so important that you make *things* paramount in your celebration. Desire the right tree, the perfect gift, the largest turkey, the right amount of snow and so on. Fret about the length of the tinsel. Make Christmas a living hell for those around you because you want it to be just right.

Whatever you do, never let it enter your mind that Christmas is for anyone else but you. Do not seek to give, but to receive.

Action Point: Write a sentence that tells the true meaning of Christmas. Remember to put in all the things you want this year.

Habit #66

Fill Your
Life with Noise

*P*ASCAL SAID, "Uh . . ." Well, I'm really not sure what the quote is and I'm too lazy to look it up, but the gist of it was that inside each of us is a vacuum, not the Eureka or Bissell kind but a hole that must be filled by something. Ineffective believers seek to fill that hole with noise.

Noise comes from many sources, but chiefly the media. Fill your days with endless chatter and information from the radio, television, videos, games and CD-ROM. As you travel from room to room you should always seek to have something *on*. Wake to a clock radio and keep one in the shower as well (battery-powered only—we want you ineffective, not deceased).

When you enter your car, flip on the radio or plug in a tape. Pretty soon you will become accustomed to having this background always with you, and you will feel uncomfortable without it. Invest in a good headset that stays with you at all times.

Keep the noise going at parties, before church begins and especially when you are in the same room with your children. If there is no noise to buoy your relationships, you are more likely to begin deep conversations and get to know each other on a new level. The noise keeps people at a distance and, best of all, keeps you from thinking about God.

Action Point: What noise do you hear right now as you are reading this book? Do you hear the radio? the air conditioner? television? If not, quickly turn something on before you have a deep thought.

Habit #67

Be a Poor Receiver

*T*HERE IS NOTHING more exasperating for people in the church than a person who will not take anything, will not receive from others and will only give. If you are such a person I applaud you, for it means that in your zeal you are being ineffective.

When someone kindly offers to watch your children and give you a break for a few hours, do not accept. Laugh and tell them how much you love your kids and how you can't stand spending time without them. If the person persists, let your children go for forty-five minutes then keep your friend's children for two weeks in the dead of winter.

If you have a specific need, like hospitalization, do not let anyone cook meals for you. Insist that you can make it on your own and shun the goodness of others. In fact, you might pick up a few gifts to distribute on your way home from intensive care.

Over time, if you learn the art of not accepting anything from others, you will subtly convey the notion that you are not weak like common folk. You have pulled yourself up by your bootstraps and will continue to do so. Feel proud when people say, "I don't think she'd even let someone bury her."

You may believe you do not deserve to be helped. You may think there are so many people with bigger problems that you don't want to enjoy the fruits of God's grace given by others. Whatever the reason, by not accepting gifts you thwart the joy your friends get in giving and hoard it all to yourself.

Habit Thought: A gift spurned each day keeps grace away.

Habit #68

Make Your Spouse Meet All Your Needs

As with coming to God, an ineffective Christian marries for one reason: to get his or her needs met. The following four attitudes will make your marriage all it shouldn't be.

1. The deep need of every person is companionship. You do not want to be lonely for the rest of your life, so you should marry. Make your spouse ease that deep need in your soul.

2. Intimacy takes many forms. Closeness, tenderness and sex are all aspects of it. However, you must believe that such things are for your gratification alone and that the person you are married to exists to make you feel satisfied.

3. Each person needs security. We want to know that financially, physically and emotionally we can depend on someone. However, the ineffective believer clings to his or her spouse like a ball and chain and feels secure only when the other is present.

4. Ultimately you must look to your spouse to meet your spiritual needs. When the other is attuned to God, you are as well. Likewise, when the other is in a religious funk, your relationship with God is in the pits.

In healthy marriages these four areas work to build a relationship, forging an unbreakable bond. But the ineffective marriage looks like host and parasite, one sucking the life from the other. If you rely on your spouse to meet all your needs, you will make both of your lives miserable in the end. After all, you have put a mere mortal in the place where only God belongs.

Action Point: In what ways have you made your spouse

meet your needs? What new ways can you find to exploit him or her today?

Habit #69

Make Worship Optional

I HAVE ALREADY touched on several issues of the spiritual life, like prayer and fasting, Bible reading and evangelism, but one of the best secrets for ineffective living is the habit of making worship optional.

I am not talking about sporadic church attendance, though that does help. I am speaking about your attitude, your outlook, the very core of your being. I am speaking about what goes through your mind when you read a passage of Scripture or see a natural wonder in creation. I am dealing with your reaction to topics like God's love, his grace, forgiveness and holiness.

For committed Christians it is impossible to look at Scripture or a sunrise and not worship God from the depth of the soul. It is impossible to ponder God's holiness without a sense of wonder and awe. But I encourage you to think of worship as something you do only when you are singing in a formal service. Worship should not be a minute-by-minute lauding of a loving God, but a few sentences of responsive reading you do every third week.

Think of worship as a nebulous add-on, a holy option. You read your Bible, study a few verses, sing a few songs, and at some point in all of those activities you worship, though you're really not sure where. Convince yourself that worship can't be planned, it just has to happen. In this way worship becomes an event rather than a lifestyle.

Questions to Ponder: When was the last time you felt you

really worshiped God? How can you avoid such an experience in the future?

Habit #70

Keep a Religious Scorecard

VITAL TO THE ineffective believer is a plumb line, a measuring stick for spirituality, for if you are to truly embrace mediocrity you must be able to keep a religious scorecard.

Keeping such a record, which is a euphemism for living by the law, not only will make you feel better about the way you live but will keep you above others you seek to compete with.

For example, if you go to a church that has Sunday-morning, Sunday-evening and Wednesday-night services, you score higher on the spiritual Richter scale than those whose church has only a Sunday-morning service and small groups. Even if you don't attend all the services at your church, you rank higher because you look better.

Give yourself points for having the right translation of the Bible. Wear conservative colors and culottes and judge those who are seen in jeans. Length of hair, absence of makeup, and a car with religious slogans all add to your total.

Whatever is outward, whatever looks good, whatever seems spiritual on the surface, seek after these things and you will be living by the law. It is imperative that you not lean on scriptural principles for your spiritual criterion, but look to your own inner sense of what is right. This will keep you and those around you basking in ineffective living for years to come.

Thought for the Day: A religious scorecard is kept for only one reason: to win.

Habit #71

Put God in a Box

YOUR CONCEPT OF God has a great deal to do with the way you live your life. This is why you must limit God or put him in a box.

Two extremes are prevalent in the church today, so I suggest you gravitate toward one of them. The first way to put God in a box is to demand that he obey you. If someone you know has an illness, command God to heal her. If you are short on cash, pray earnestly for money to drop into your lap. In this extreme God is simply the heavenly valet you order from task to task.

By using this method you imply the belief that God revolves around you and is there to glorify you. Angels are at your beck and call; visions, tongues and all manner of miracles are yours.

Another excellent way to put God in a box is to deny the Almighty the ability to work in people's lives. Anything that smells of the miraculous must be discarded because "I don't think God works that way anymore." If someone experiences a life-changing event you've never had, explain that they are mistaken and repeat the phrase "He only did that in the first century."

As much as you are able, make God conform to your image and what you believe he ought to be like. Do not leave room for him to act in any way he pleases. Believe he must first ask your permission.

Thoughts to Ponder: What boxes have you put God in lately? What would happen if you didn't put him in a box?

Habit #72

Hold Grudges

*L*IKE THE ELEPHANT, the ineffective Christian finds it hard to forget things, particularly the unpleasant ones. If you are to remain lukewarm in your faith, you must learn the fine art of holding grudges.

Of course a good grudge is one that is aged in anger, festering in the soul over many years. This could be a grudge you had against a classmate, teacher or bus driver from childhood.

But I find the best grudges, the ones that really debilitate your faith, are ones held against others in the church family. These could be instances where you were intentionally or unintentionally treated badly.

First tell yourself you have the right to be angry. This is the "mull" stage. Then move from the mull to active hatred. Begin thinking of terrible things you'd like to do to that person or their family members. The third stage is "holding." A grudge does you no harm unless you continually pull it out, poke it, prod it or mentally play with it.

Under no circumstances should you forgive the other person. You should never think, *God has forgiven me so much, I should not hold this against them any longer.* Stay away from the concept of grace and make them pay for what they did! The more grudges you can hold at the same time, the more ineffective you'll become.

Action Point: Think of someone who did you wrong many years ago. Now grit your teeth. Imagine them being embarrassed in a social situation. Smile. Repeat the process.

Habit #73

Approach Church like a Consumer

*C*OMMITTED Christians know the value of a good church. They desire worship, see needs, plug in, help out, get involved. However, ineffective Christians do not look for ways to serve, but for ways to change things for their own good.

You must approach church like a consumer. Hop from one congregation to the next, keeping a careful list of positives and negatives such as: Church A's pastor preaches only fifteen minutes, but the refreshments at Church B are always fresher. Church C has a splendid sound system that never squeals, while Church D has a paved parking lot.

Do not judge a church by how much people love each other and are committed to discipleship. Do not judge a church by the ability of the pastor to teach God's Word. You must judge a church by your own selective criteria and choose a place of worship as you would a loaf of bread or a dishwashing detergent. You must judge a church by how it makes you feel when you walk out the door on Sunday morning.

A good approach is to not decide on a place of worship. Keep the pastor and the congregation in a state of limbo about your involvement. Say things like "We're not sure we want to go here because we don't think the youth group would be right if we started having kids."

If you have been living in an area for more than a year and still haven't found a church, good job!

Thought to Ponder: Remember, the church exists for one reason, to please you.

Habit #74

Never Drink
from Living Water

*I*F YOU FOLLOW THE habits listed so far in this book, you will probably not have a problem with Habit #74. But perhaps you will come to a point in your spiritual life where you desire more than anything to know God. Remote as the possibility may seem, there may be a time when your heart will cry out to God and you will thirst for him with an unquenchable passion and desire him above all else.

If this ever happens to you, and you still want to remain ineffective, remember to drink from temporal waters and not the living water. In order to do this you must follow the single biggest "Do Not" of the ineffective Christian.

DO NOT READ THE BIBLE.

Follow your inner voice. Read books that offer easy steps to fulfillment. You can even read what others say about the Bible, but under no circumstances are you to read the Bible.

You must seek to drink from temporal waters, leaning on counselors, friends, your job, television or a time-management guru. Lean on anything that will take the ache in your soul away from you, but do not read the Bible.

Reading the Bible is dangerous because a transformation takes place when you put yourself under the spotlight of God's Word. You see your sin. You see your need for God. You will yearn for him and him alone. If you begin reading the Bible for yourself, pretty soon nothing will satisfy you until you know God intimately.

Scripture to Avoid: John 7:37-38

Habit #75

Guide Others with Guilt

*G*UILT IS A RATHER sensitive topic. But lukewarm Christians must realize that guilt can help maximize their ineffectiveness and spread it to others.

Think of guilt as cholesterol. Some of it is good for your diet; much of it is bad. In the same way good guilt causes you to cast yourself on the mercy of God. It pushes you toward repentance and forgiveness. Bad guilt is something you use on other people to motivate and manipulate. You, of course, should use bad guilt.

For example, if you are given the task of recruiting Sunday-school teachers, you must not pray earnestly and ask God to take control of the situation; you must grab guilt by the horns and wrack people's lives with it. Say things like "I'd like you to consider teaching our third-graders this year—that is, unless you don't think children are important," or, "I saw you going to a ballgame the other night. It's a shame you couldn't spend half that time to prepare a lesson for the kids in our sixth-grade class."

If others do not respond to your call on their lives, make them feel guilty. Bring up their past wrongs, shame them and urge them to do what you want in order to make God like them again. If they still refuse, knit your brow, fold your arms and sternly say, "I'll be praying that God will change your heart."

Guilt is the best motivator for the ineffective Christian. Use it today to your best advantage.

Bumper Sticker: Have you made a friend feel guilty today?

Habit #76

Look for Significance in All the Wrong Places

*E*ACH PERSON ON Planet Earth longs to be known, to be heard, to make a difference. We want our lives to be significant. This is a God-given desire. However, you must look for significance in all the wrong places.

First, look for it in people. The more well-known people you can say you know, the more significant you will be. The number of autographed copies of successful books and phone numbers of important people you possess correlates to a life of significance.

But don't stop there. Look for significance in things. Get your feeling of worth from the amount of money you make, the number of rungs you've progressed in your company, how close your personal parking space is to the front door. Cars, clothes, houses, books published and even plush carpeting are all valid "significance builders."

To be honest, it doesn't really matter where you look for significance as long as you do not look for it in your relationship with God. It is valid, of course, to work for God's favor, to compare your spiritual accomplishments to those of others in order to gain significance. But your significance should never be based on the premise that God loves you and you are his child. Never let yourself rest in the fact that you are a son or daughter of the King of Kings and that God could not love you more than he does this very moment.

Action Point: Whose name can you drop today to make others feel you are important?

Habit #77

Don't Finish
What You Start

*G*ROWING CHRISTIANS learn that it is vital to complete tasks they believe God has given them. But the ineffective Christian discovers how good it is to begin many things but finish just a few.

One great place to start is Bible reading. I suggest you promise to read the entire Bible in the next year, then stop somewhere between Adam and Moses.

Small groups are the bane of ineffective Christians since they promote personal growth and accountability. Begin going to such a group, then drop out after two or three meetings because you're "overextended."

Commit yourself to any number of church committees and fail to fulfill your obligation. Teach a Sunday-school class for half a quarter. Write half of an encouraging letter to a missionary, then abandon it because you aren't sure where you put the address.

The most important thin

Editor's note: We are very sorry the author did not get us the complete manuscript in time for publication, but we feel he has illustrated his point by example nicely.

Ineffective Christianity: A Personal Test

This helpful scientific exam will aid you in evaluating your spiritual state of being. Please answer each question as honestly as possible, circling the appropriate letter. Ineffective answers are listed immediately following the test.

1. The Bible is . . .
    a. my guide.
    b. the "Good Book."
    c. on the coffee table under the newspaper. (Or try the car or maybe the magazine rack. It's around, I saw it last week.)

2. People know I'm a Christian because . . .
    a. I love God with all my being and others as myself.
    b. I go to church every Sunday, except when there's a really big game on.
    c. There's a fish symbol on my car.

3. I've talked to someone about Christ . . .
    a. in the last week.
    b. in the last year.
    c. in the last decade, if you count saying "God bless you" to someone who sneezed in the doctor's office.

4. When faced with a moral or ethical dilemma I . . .
    a. try to find Scripture that sheds light on the subject.
    b. pray and seek godly counsel.
    c. toss a coin and cross my fingers.

5. The biggest priorities in life in order are . . .

    a. God, my family, my work.

    b. my family, God, my work.

    c. my work, my family, my stamp collection, my part-time business, my computer, God.

6. I determine how much I will give to my church by . . .

    a. a percentage of my gross income.

    b. a percentage of my _____ income.

    c. how much change I happen to have with me.

7. Communion is meaningful for me because . . .

    a. I celebrate the death, burial and resurrection of Christ.

    b. I reflect on my sins and spend time confessing them before God.

    c. it's always at the end of the service and that means I'm only ten minutes from lunch.

8. Spiritual warfare is . . .

    a. something important I'm aware of.

    b. something going on in the heavenlies.

    c. something Frank Peretti made a lot of money writing about.

9. The ultimate goal for my life is . . .

    a. to hear God say, "Well done, faithful servant."

    b. to lead others to Christ by my words and my example.

    c. to be happy.

10. True joy comes from . . .

    a. a close relationship with God.

    b. a close relationship with other people.

    c. being left alone by God and other people.

Answers

1. c. (True ineffective Christians have no idea where to find their Bible.)

2. b and c. (Fish symbols and other paraphernalia exempt you from saying or doing anything about your faith.)

3. c.

4. c. (Some people think there's a verse for everything, and that's just not true.)

5. c. (Your computer may be higher on the list.)

6. c. (The trick is not making the offering plate jangle with your dimes and nickels.)

7. c. (Isn't it a great feeling to know your weekly obligation is almost over?)

8. c.

9. c. (What else is there?)

10. c. (True ineffectiveness can be achieved only in isolation.)

WESTMINSTER PUBLIC LIBRARY
3031 WEST 76th AVE.
WESTMINSTER, CO 80030